A Holy Hour Companion

A Holy Hour Companion

Prayer ✠ Scripture ✠ Reflection ✠ Ritual

Compiled by
John T. Kyler

Introduction by
Timothy P. O'Malley

LITURGICAL PRESS
Collegeville, Minnesota

www.litpress.org

Cover design by Savanah N. Landerholm.

1 2 3 4 5 6 7 8 9

Library of Congress Control Number: 2023940215

ISBN: 979-8-4008-0060-3

Contents

II. The Witness of Holy Women and Men

III. Litany of the Holy Eucharist

IV. Psalmody

V. Additional Scripture

Introduction

The Holy Hour: What Are We Made For?

In my office, when people ask someone how things are going, the near universal response is: "I'm busy." In asking this question, I presume that my co-workers are not really performing an investigation of their colleague's calendar. And yet, we tend to think about our well-being in terms of what we are doing.

This tendency is rather detrimental to happiness. We are not reducible to our calendar. Rather, we are made for relationships with friends and family members. We are made to ponder the great questions of life. We are made to be free.

A Holy Hour before the Blessed Sacrament is a religious practice that reminds us what we are made for. In the busyness of a day, we take an hour to spend time before the Eucharistic presence of Jesus Christ. The

Blessed Sacrament does not need to be exposed. Even to sit before the tabernacle in silence is worth it.

And in such silence, we discover anew what we are made for. Pausing to give thanks to Jesus hidden under the sign of bread is a prophetic act. It is a healing act. I am not reducible to what I do, but instead, I am beloved by the Lord of heaven and earth simply because I am. God loves me. And in that quiet moment, I can share with my beloved God the deepest joys and sorrows of my life.

We can, of course, speak to God directly every moment of every day. But there is a particular intimacy to spending time with the hidden presence of love in the Eucharist. Before the tabernacle or monstrance, God is present before me. God wants to be with me. And God wants nothing more than my presence. Not to plan an elaborate practice of prayer. Just to sit in silence and love before the God who is love.

If you take this hour to be with God, you will find all sorts of hidden joys. At Mass, you'll more deeply appreciate the sacrifice of love that you are to offer upon the altar alongside the bread and wine. You'll start to notice the ways that divine love comes to you each day. You'll notice the hidden Christ who comes to you in the hungry and thirsty.

So the next time you have a chance, sit before the Eucharistic Lord and let him ask you, "How are you doing?" This God of ours really wants to know.

Dr. Timothy P. O'Malley

The Practice of Meditation

Meditation is spiritual work, sometimes difficult work. But it is a work of love and of desire. It is not something that can be practiced without effort, at least in the beginning. And the sincerity, humility and perseverance of our efforts will be proportionate to our desire. This desire in turn is a gift of grace. Anyone who imagines [they] can simply begin meditating without praying for the desire and the grace to do so, will soon give up. But the desire to meditate, and the grace to begin meditating, should be taken as an implicit promise of further graces. In meditation, as in everything else in the Christian life, everything depends on our correspondence with the grace of the Holy Spirit.

Meditation is almost all contained in this one idea: the idea of *awakening* our interior self and attuning ourselves inwardly to the Holy Spirit, so that we will be able to respond to His grace. In mental prayer, over the years, we must allow our interior perceptivity to be refined and purified. We must attune ourselves to unexpected movements of grace, which do not fit our own preconceived ideas of the spiritual life at all, and which in no way flatter our own ambitious aspirations.

We must be ready to cooperate not only with graces that console, but with graces that humiliate us. Not only with lights that exalt us, but with lights that blast our self-complacency. Much of our coldness and dryness in prayer may well be a kind of unconscious defense against grace. Without realizing it, we allow our nature to desensitize our souls so that we cannot perceive graces which we intuitively foresee may prove to be painful.

Meditation is then always to be associated in practice with abandonment to the will and action of God. It goes hand in hand with self-renunciation and with obedience to the Holy Spirit. Meditation that does not seek to bring our whole being into conformity with God's will must naturally remain sterile and abstract. But any sincere interior prayer that really seeks this one all important end—our conformity to God's will in our regard—cannot fail to be rewarded by grace. It will prove, without question, to be one of the most sanctifying forces in our lives.

And St. Teresa of Avila believed that no one who was faithful to the practice of meditation could possibly lose [their] soul.

Thomas Merton

I. Traditional Prayers of the Church

1

The Lord's Prayer (Our Father)

Our Father, who art in heaven,
hallowed be thy name;
thy kingdom come,
thy will be done
on earth as it is in heaven.
Give us this day our daily bread,
and forgive us our trespasses,
as we forgive those who trespass against us;
and lead us not into temptation,
but deliver us from evil.

For the kingdom,
the power and the glory are yours
now and forever.

✠

2

The Hail Mary

Hail, Mary, full of grace, the Lord is with you.
Blessed are you among women,
and blessed is the fruit of your womb, Jesus.
Holy Mary, Mother of God, pray for us sinners,
now and at the hour of our death. Amen.

3

Doxology

Glory to the Father, and to the Son, and to the Holy Spirit,
As it was in the beginning, is now, and will be forever. Amen.

✠

4

Soul of Christ (Anima Christi)

Soul of Christ, sanctify me
Body of Christ, save me
Blood of Christ, inebriate me
Water from the side of Christ, wash me
Passion of Christ, strengthen me
O good Jesus, hear me
Within your wounds, hide me
Suffer me not to be separated from you
From the malignant enemy defend me
In the hour of my death call me
And bid me come unto you
That with your saints I may praise you forever and ever.
Amen.

5

Morning Prayer: Canticle of Zechariah (Luke 1:68-79)

Blessed be the Lord God of Israel:
for he has visited his people and redeemed them;
he has raised up for us a horn of salvation
in the House of David his servant,
as he spoke through the mouth of his holy ones,
his prophets from ages past:

To grant salvation from our foes,
and from the hand of all who hate us,
showing mercy to our fathers,
remembering his holy covenant,
the oath he swore to Abraham our father;

To grant that, freed from the hand of our foes,
we may serve him without fear
in holiness and righteousness
all the days of our life.

And you, little child, will be called
the Prophet of the Most High,
for you will go before the Lord
to make ready his ways:
to grant knowledge of salvation to his people
by the forgiveness of their sins;

Through the tender mercy of our God,
the Dawn from on high will visit us,
to shine on those who sit in darkness,
and those in the shadow of death;
to guide our feet into the way of peace.

6

Evening Prayer: Canticle of Mary (Luke 1:46-55)

My soul proclaims the greatness of the Lord,
and my spirit rejoices in God my Savior,
for he has looked upon his handmaid in her
lowliness;
for behold, from this day forward,
all generations will call me blessed.

For the Almighty has done great things for me,
and holy is his name.
His mercy is from age to age
for those who fear him.

He has made known the strength of his arm,
and has scattered the proud in their conceit of heart.
He has cast down the mighty from their thrones
and has exalted those who are lowly.
He has filled the hungry with good things,
and has sent the rich away empty.

He has helped his servant Israel,
mindful of his mercy,
even as he promised to our fathers,
to Abraham and his descendants forever.

✠

7

Night Prayer: Canticle of Simeon (Luke 2:29-32)

Now you dismiss your servant in peace,
according to your word, O Master;

For my eyes have seen your salvation,
which you prepared in the sight of all the peoples:

A light for revelation to the nations,
and the glory of your people Israel.

✠

8

Penitential Prayer

O God, most merciful Father,
like the Prodigal Son, I turn to you and say:
I have sinned against you;
I am no longer worthy to be called your child.

O Jesus Christ, Savior of the world,
like the thief to whom you opened the gates of
Paradise, I beg you:
Lord, remember me in your Kingdom.

O Holy Spirit, fount of love,
with trust I call upon you:
Purify me;
make me walk as a child of the light.

✠

9

Tantum Ergo

Down in adoration falling,
Lo! the sacred Host we hail;
Lo! o'er ancient forms departing,
Newer rites of grace prevail;
Faith for all defects supplying,
Where the feeble senses fail.
To the everlasting Father,
And the Son who reigns on high,
With the Holy Spirit proceeding
Forth from each eternally,
Be salvation, honor, blessing,
Might and endless majesty. Amen.

℣. You have given them bread from heaven,

℟. Having all delight within it.

Let us pray.

O God, who in this wonderful Sacrament
left us a memorial of your Passion:

grant, we implore you,
that we may so venerate
the sacred mysteries of your Body and Blood,
as always to be conscious of the fruit of your
Redemption.
You who live and reign forever and ever. Amen.

✠

10

The Divine Praises

Blessed be God.
Blessed be his holy Name.
Blessed be Jesus Christ, true God and true Man.
Blessed be the name of Jesus.
Blessed be his most Sacred Heart.
Blessed be his most Precious Blood.
Blessed be Jesus in the most holy Sacrament of the altar.
Blessed be the Holy Spirit, the Paraclete.
Blessed be the great Mother of God, Mary most holy.
Blessed be her holy and Immaculate Conception.
Blessed be her glorious Assumption.
Blessed be the name of Mary, Virgin and Mother.
Blessed be Saint Joseph, her most chaste spouse.
Blessed be God in his angels and in his saints.

✠

11

Prayers before the Eucharist

Lord,
may this sacrament of new life
warm our hearts with your love
and make us eager
for the eternal joy of your kingdom.
We ask this through Christ our Lord.

Lord our God,
in this great sacrament
we come into the presence of Jesus Christ, your Son,
born of the Virgin Mary
and crucified for our salvation.
May we who declare our faith in this fountain of
love and mercy
drink from it the water of everlasting life.
We ask this through Christ, our Lord.

Lord,
give to our hearts
the light of faith and the fire of love,
that we may worship in spirit and truth
our God and Lord, present in this sacrament,
who lives and reigns forever and ever.

II. The Witness of Holy Women and Men

12

May the Lord Support Us (Saint Cardinal John Henry Newman)

May the Lord support us all the day long,
Till the shade of day lengthens and the evening
comes,
and the busy world is hushed,
and the fever of life is over,
and our work is done.
Then in his mercy may he give us a safe lodging,
and holy rest, and peace at the last.

✠

13

God Has Called Us (Sister Thea Bowman, FSPA)

God has called us to speak the word that is Christ,
that is truth, that is salvation.
And if we speak that word in love and faith,
with patience and prayer and perseverance, it will
take root.
It does have power to save us.
Call one another!
Testify!
Teach!
Act on the Word!
Witness!

14

My God, I Am Yours (Venerable Catherine McAuley)

My God, I am yours for time and eternity.
Teach me to cast myself entirely
into the arms of your loving Providence
with a lively, unlimited confidence in your
compassionate, tender pity.
Grant, O merciful Redeemer,
That whatever you ordain or permit may be
acceptable to me.
Take from my heart all painful anxiety;
let nothing sadden me but sin,
nothing delight me but the hope of coming to the
possession of You
my God and my all, in your everlasting kingdom.
Amen.

15

Lord, Make Me an Instrument of Your Peace (Attributed to Saint Francis of Assisi)

Lord, make me an instrument of your peace:
where there is hatred, let me sow love;
where there is injury, pardon;
where there is doubt, faith;
where there is despair; hope;
where there is darkness, light;
and where there is sadness, joy.

O Divine Master, grant that I may not so much seek
to be consoled as to console,
to be understood as to understand,
to be loved as to love.
For it is in giving that we receive,
it is in pardoning that we are pardoned,
and it is in dying that we are born to eternal life.

16

All Shall Be Well (Julian of Norwich)

All shall be well,
and all shall be well,
and all manner of things shall be well.

✠

17

Christ, Be with Me (Saint Patrick's Breastplate)

Christ, be with me,
Christ before me,
Christ behind me,
Christ in me,
Christ beneath me,
Christ above me,
Christ on my right,
Christ on my left,
Christ where I lie,
Christ where I sit,
Christ where I arise,
Christ in the heart of everyone who thinks of me,
Christ in the heart of everyone who speaks of me,
Christ in every eye that sees me,
Christ in every ear that hears me.

18

Christ Has No Body Now but Yours (Attributed to Saint Teresa of Ávila)

Christ has no body now but yours.
No hands, no feet on earth but yours.
Yours are the eyes through which he looks
compassion on this world.
Yours are the feet with which he walks to do good.
Yours are the hands with which he blesses all the
world.

Yours are the hands,
Yours are the feet,
Yours are the eyes,
Yours are his body.
Christ has no body now on earth but yours.

19

Prophets of a Future Not Our Own (Bishop Kenneth Untener, Often Attributed to Saint Archbishop Oscar Romero)

It helps, now and then, to step back and take a long view.
The kingdom is not only beyond our efforts, it is even beyond our vision.
We accomplish in our lifetime only a tiny fraction of the magnificent
enterprise that is God's work. Nothing we do is complete, which is a way of
saying that the Kingdom always lies beyond us.
No statement says all that could be said.
No prayer fully expresses our faith.
No confession brings perfection.
No pastoral visit brings wholeness.
No program accomplishes the Church's mission.
No set of goals and objectives includes everything.
This is what we are about.

We plant the seeds that one day will grow.
We water seeds already planted, knowing that they hold future promise.
We lay foundations that will need further development.
We provide yeast that produces far beyond our capabilities.
We cannot do everything, and there is a sense of liberation in realizing that.
This enables us to do something, and to do it very well.
It may be incomplete, but it is a beginning, a step along the way, an
opportunity for the Lord's grace to enter and do the rest.
We may never see the end results, but that is the difference between the master
builder and the worker.
We are workers, not master builders; ministers, not messiahs.
We are prophets of a future not our own.

✠

20

Take, Lord, Receive (Saint Ignatius of Loyola)

Take, Lord, receive all my liberty,
my memory,
my understanding,
my whole will,
all that I have and all that I possess.
You gave it all to me, Lord; I give it all back to you.
Do with it as you will, according to your good
pleasure.
Give me your love and your grace,
for with this I have all that I need.

21

Fall in Love (Joseph Whelan, SJ, Often Attributed to Father Pedro Arrupe, SJ)

Nothing is more practical than
finding God, than
falling in Love
in a quite absolute, final way.

What you are in love with,
what seizes your imagination,
will affect everything.

It will decide
what will get you out of bed in the morning,
what you do with your evenings,
how you spend your weekends,
what you read,
whom you know,
what breaks your heart,
and what amazes you with joy and gratitude.

Fall in Love,
stay in love,
and it will decide everything.

III. Litany of the Holy Eucharist

22

Litany of the Holy Eucharist

Lord, have mercy	Lord, have mercy
Christ, have mercy	Christ, have mercy
Lord, have mercy	Lord, have mercy
Jesus, the Most High	have mercy on us
Jesus, the holy One	have mercy on us
Jesus, Word of God	have mercy on us
Jesus, only Son of the Father	have mercy on us
Jesus, Son of Mary	have mercy on us
Jesus, crucified for us	have mercy on us
Jesus, risen from the dead	have mercy on us
Jesus, reigning in glory	have mercy on us
Jesus, coming in glory	have mercy on us
Jesus, our Lord	have mercy on us
Jesus, our hope	have mercy on us
Jesus, our peace	have mercy on us
Jesus, our Savior	have mercy on us
Jesus, our salvation	have mercy on us
Jesus, our resurrection	have mercy on us

Jesus, Judge of all	have mercy on us
Jesus, Lord of the Church	have mercy on us
Jesus, Lord of creation	have mercy on us
Jesus, Lover of all	have mercy on us
Jesus, life of the world	have mercy on us
Jesus, freedom for the imprisoned	have mercy on us
Jesus, joy of the sorrowing	have mercy on us
Jesus, giver of the Spirit	have mercy on us
Jesus, giver of good gifts	have mercy on us
Jesus, source of new life	have mercy on us
Jesus, Lord of life	have mercy on us
Jesus, eternal high priest	have mercy on us
Jesus, priest and victim	have mercy on us
Jesus, true Shepherd	have mercy on us
Jesus, true Light	have mercy on us

Jesus, bread of heaven	have mercy on us
Jesus, bread of life	have mercy on us
Jesus, bread of thanksgiving	have mercy on us
Jesus, life-giving bread	have mercy on us
Jesus, holy manna	have mercy on us

Jesus, new covenant — have mercy on us
Jesus, food for everlasting life — have mercy on us
Jesus, food for our journey — have mercy on us
Jesus, holy banquet — have mercy on us
Jesus, true sacrifice — have mercy on us
Jesus, perfect sacrifice — have mercy on us
Jesus, eternal sacrifice — have mercy on us
Jesus, divine Victim — have mercy on us
Jesus, Mediator of the new covenant — have mercy on us
Jesus, mystery of the altar — have mercy on us
Jesus, medicine of immortality — have mercy on us
Jesus, pledge of eternal glory — have mercy on us

Jesus, Lamb of God, you take away the sins of the world: have mercy on us
Jesus, Bearer of our sins, you take away the sins of the world: have mercy on us
Jesus, Redeemer of the world, you take away the sins of the world: have mercy on us

Christ, hear us — Christ, hear us
Christ, graciously hear us — Christ, graciously hear us

Lord Jesus, hear our prayer — Lord Jesus, hear our prayer

✠

IV. Psalmody

23

Psalm 23: The Lord Is My Shepherd

The Lord is my shepherd;
there is nothing I shall want.
Fresh and green are the pastures
where he gives me repose.
Near restful waters he leads me;
he revives my soul.

He guides me along the right path,
for the sake of his name.
Though I should walk in the valley of the shadow
of death,
no evil would I fear, for you are with me.
Your crook and your staff will give me comfort.

You have prepared a table before me
in the sight of my foes.
My head you have anointed with oil;
my cup is overflowing.

Surely goodness and mercy shall follow me
all the days of my life.
In the LORD's own house shall I dwell
for length of days unending.

✠

24

Psalm 27:
The Lord Is My Light and My Salvation

The Lord is my light and my salvation;
whom should I fear?
The Lord is the stronghold of my life;
whom should I dread? . . .

There is one thing I ask of the Lord,
only this do I seek:
to live in the house of the Lord
all the days of my life,
to gaze on the beauty of the Lord,
to inquire at his temple. . . .

O Lord, hear my voice when I call;
have mercy and answer me.
Of you my heart has spoken,
"Seek his face." . . .

25

Psalm 34:
Taste and See the Goodness of the Lord

I will bless the LORD at all times,
praise of him is always in my mouth.
In the LORD my soul shall make its boast;
the humble shall hear and be glad.

Glorify the LORD with me;
together let us praise his name.
I sought the LORD, and he answered me;
from all my terrors he set me free.

Look toward him and be radiant;
let your faces not be abashed.
The lowly one called; the LORD heard,
and rescued him from all his distress.

The angel of the LORD is encamped
around those who fear him, to rescue them.
Taste and see that the LORD is good.
Blessed the man who seeks refuge in him. . . .

26

Psalm 51: Have Mercy on Me, O God

Have mercy on me, O God,
according to your merciful love;
according to your great compassion,
blot out my transgressions.
Wash me completely from my iniquity,
and cleanse me from my sin.

My transgressions, truly I know them;
my sin is always before me.
Against you, you alone, have I sinned;
what is evil in your sight I have done.
So you are just in your sentence,
without reproach in your judgment.

Behold, in guilt I was born,
a sinner when my mother conceived me.
Behold, you delight in sincerity of heart;
in secret you teach me wisdom.
Cleanse me with hyssop, and I shall be pure;
wash me, and I shall be whiter than snow.

Let me hear rejoicing and gladness,
that the bones you have crushed may exult.
Turn away your face from my sins,
and blot out all my guilt.

Create a pure heart for me, O God;
renew a steadfast spirit within me.
Do not cast me away from your presence;
take not your holy spirit from me.

Restore in me the joy of your salvation;
sustain in me a willing spirit.
I will teach transgressors your ways,
that sinners may return to you.

Rescue me from bloodshed, O God,
O God of my salvation,
and then my tongue shall ring out your justice.
O Lord, open my lips
and my mouth shall proclaim your praise.

For in sacrifice you take no delight;
burnt offering from me would not please you.
My sacrifice to God, a broken spirit:

a broken and humbled heart,
you will not spurn, O God.

In your good pleasure, show favor to Zion;
rebuild the walls of Jerusalem.
Then you will delight in right sacrifice,
burnt offerings wholly consumed.
Then you will be offered young bulls on your altar.

✠

27

Psalm 139:
I Praise You, for I Am Wonderfully Made

O Lord, you search me and you know me.
You yourself know my resting and my rising;
you discern my thoughts from afar.
You mark when I walk or lie down;
you know all my ways through and through. . . .

For it was you who formed my inmost being,
knit me together in my mother's womb.
I thank you who wonderfully made me;
how wonderful are your works,
which my soul knows well!

My frame was not hidden from you,
when I was being fashioned in secret
and molded in the depths of the earth. . . .

V. Additional Scripture

28

Isaiah 55:1-2 — All You Who Are Thirsty, Come

All you who are thirsty,
come to the water!
You who have no money,
    come, buy grain and eat;
Come, buy grain without money,
    wine and milk without cost!
Why spend your money for what is not bread;
    your wages for what does not satisfy?
Only listen to me, and you shall eat well,
    you shall delight in rich fare.

29

Ezekiel 36:24-28 — I Will Give You a New Heart

I will take you away from among the nations, gather you from all the lands, and bring you back to your own soil. I will sprinkle clean water over you to make you clean; from all your impurities and from all your idols I will cleanse you. I will give you a new heart, and a new spirit I will put within you. I will remove the heart of stone from your flesh and give you a heart of flesh. I will put my spirit within you so that you walk in my statutes, observe my ordinances, and keep them. You will live in the land I gave to your ancestors; you will be my people, and I will be your God.

30

Micah 6:8 — Walk Humbly with Your God

You have been told, O mortal, what is good,
    and what the LORD requires of you:
Only to do justice and to love goodness,
    and to walk humbly with your God.

✠

31

1 Corinthians 10:16-17 — The Bread Is One and We Are One Body

The cup of blessing that we bless, is it not a participation in the blood of Christ? The bread that we break, is it not a participation in the body of Christ? Because the loaf of bread is one, we, though many, are one body, for we all partake of the one loaf.

✠

32

1 Corinthians 10:31–11:1 — Do Everything for the Glory of God

So whether you eat or drink, or whatever you do, do everything for the glory of God. Avoid giving offense, whether to Jews or Greeks or the church of God, just as I try to please everyone in every way, not seeking my own benefit but that of the many, that they may be saved. Be imitators of me, as I am of Christ.

33

1 John 4:7-12 — God Remains in Us

Beloved, let us love one another, because love is of God; everyone who loves is begotten by God and knows God. Whoever is without love does not know God, for God is love. In this way the love of God was revealed to us: God sent his only Son into the world so that we might have life through him.
In this is love: not that we have loved God, but that he loved us and sent his Son as expiation for our sins.
Beloved, if God so loved us, we must also love one another. No one has ever seen God. Yet, if we love one another, God remains in us, and his love is brought to perfection in us.

34

Luke 22:17-20 — Take This and Share

Then he took a cup, gave thanks, and said, "Take this and share it among yourselves; for I tell you [that] from this time on I shall not drink of the fruit of the vine until the kingdom of God comes." Then he took the bread, said the blessing, broke it, and gave it to them, saying, "This is my body, which will be given for you; do this in memory of me." And likewise the cup after they had eaten, saying, "This cup is the new covenant in my blood, which will be shed for you."

35

John 13:1-15 — Jesus Washes the Disciples' Feet

Before the feast of Passover, Jesus knew that his hour had come to pass from this world to the Father. He loved his own in the world and he loved them to the end. The devil had already induced Judas, son of Simon the Iscariot, to hand him over. So, during supper, fully aware that the Father had put everything into his power and that he had come from God and was returning to God, he rose from supper and took off his outer garments. He took a towel and tied it around his waist. Then he poured water into a basin and began to wash the disciples' feet and dry them with the towel around his waist. He came to Simon Peter, who said to him, "Master, are you going to wash my feet?" Jesus answered and said to him, "What I am doing, you do not understand now, but you will understand later." Peter said to him, "You will never wash my feet." Jesus answered him, "Unless I wash you, you will have no inheritance with me." Simon Peter said to him, "Master, then not only my feet, but my hands and head as well." Jesus said to him, "Whoever has bathed has no need except to have his feet washed, for he is clean all over; so you are clean, but not all." For he knew who would betray him; for this reason, he said, "Not all of you are clean."

So when he had washed their feet [and] put his garments back on and reclined at table again, he said to them, "Do you realize what I have done for you? You call me 'teacher' and 'master,' and rightly so, for indeed I am. If I, therefore, the master and teacher, have washed your feet, you ought to wash one another's feet. I have given you a model to follow, so that as I have done for you, you should also do."

36

Luke 24:13-35 — The Road to Emmaus

Now that very day two of them were going to a village seven miles from Jerusalem called Emmaus, and they were conversing about all the things that had occurred. And it happened that while they were conversing and debating, Jesus himself drew near and walked with them, but their eyes were prevented from recognizing him. He asked them, "What are you discussing as you walk along?" They stopped, looking downcast. One of them, named Cleopas, said to him in reply, "Are you the only visitor to Jerusalem who does not know of the things that have taken place there in these days?" And he replied to them, "What sort of things?" They said to him, "The things that happened to Jesus the Nazarene, who was a prophet mighty in deed and word before God and all the people, how our chief priests and rulers both handed him over to a sentence of death and crucified him. But we were hoping that he would be the one to redeem Israel; and besides all this, it is now the third day since this took place. Some women from our group, however, have astounded us: they were at the tomb early in the morning and did not find his body; they came back and reported that they had indeed seen a vision of angels who announced that he was alive. Then some of those with us went to the tomb and found things just as the women had described, but him they did not see." And he said to them, "Oh, how foolish you are! How slow of heart to believe all that the prophets spoke! Was it not necessary that the Messiah should suffer these things and enter into his glory?" Then beginning with Moses and all the prophets, he interpreted to them what referred to him in all the scriptures. As they approached the village to which they were going, he gave the impression that he was going on farther. But they urged him, "Stay with us, for it is nearly evening and the day is almost over." So he went in to stay with them. And it happened that, while he was with them at table, he took bread, said the blessing, broke it, and gave it to them. With that their eyes were opened and they recognized him, but he vanished from their sight. Then they said to each other, "Were not our hearts burning [within us] while he spoke to us on the way and opened the scriptures to us?" So they set out at once and returned to Jerusalem where they found gathered together the eleven and those with them who were saying, "The Lord has truly been raised and has appeared to Simon!" Then the two recounted what had taken place on the way and how he was made known to them in the breaking of the bread.

✠

37

John 21:1-14 — Jesus Gave Them Bread

After this, Jesus revealed himself again to his disciples at the Sea of Tiberias. He revealed himself in this way. Together were Simon Peter, Thomas called Didymus, Nathanael from Cana in Galilee, Zebedee's sons, and two others of his disciples. Simon Peter said to them, "I am going fishing." They said to him, "We also will come with you." So they went out and got into the boat, but that night they caught nothing. When it was already dawn, Jesus was standing on the shore; but the disciples did not realize that it was Jesus. Jesus said to them, "Children, have you caught anything to eat?" They answered him, "No." So he said to them, "Cast the net over the right side of the boat and you will find something." So they cast it, and were not able to pull it in because of the number of fish. So the disciple whom Jesus loved said to Peter, "It is the Lord." When Simon Peter heard that it was the Lord, he tucked in his garment, for he was lightly clad, and jumped into the sea. The other disciples came in the boat, for they were not far from shore, only about a hundred yards, dragging the net with the fish. When they climbed out on shore, they saw a charcoal fire with fish on it and bread. Jesus said to them, "Bring some of the fish you just caught." So Simon Peter went over and dragged the net ashore full of one hundred fifty-three large fish. Even though there were so many, the net was not torn. Jesus said to them, "Come, have breakfast." And none of the disciples dared to ask him, "Who are you?" because they realized it was the Lord. Jesus came over and took the bread and gave it to them, and in like manner the fish. This was now the third time Jesus was revealed to his disciples after being raised from the dead.

✠

38

Luke 24:36-43 — The Appearance in Jerusalem

While they were still speaking about this, [Jesus] stood in their midst and said to them, "Peace be with you." But they were startled and terrified and thought that they were seeing a ghost. Then he said to them, "Why are you troubled? And why do questions arise in your hearts? Look at my hands and my feet, that it is I myself. Touch me and see, because a ghost does not have flesh and bones as you can see I have." And as he said this, he showed them his hands and his feet. While they were still incredulous for joy and were amazed, he asked them, "Have you anything here to eat?" They gave him a piece of baked fish; he took it and ate it in front of them.

VI. Spiritual Reading

39

Excerpt from "You Are Yourselves What You Receive" by Saint Augustine

You ought to know what you have received, what you are about to receive, what you ought to receive every day. That bread which you can see on the altar, sanctified by the word of God, is the body of Christ. That cup, or rather what the cup contains, sanctified by the word of God, is the blood of Christ. It was by means of these things that the Lord Christ wished to present us with his body and blood, which he shed for our sake for the forgiveness of sins. If you receive them well, you are yourselves what you receive.

40

Excerpt from *My Sacrifice and Yours* by Virgil Michel, OSB

Not all [people] were capable of being present at the sacrifice of Calvary, and of there choosing to accept or reject the blessings of Christ's sacrifice. This sacrifice was enacted within the space of a few days; while the human race was to continue throughout all time. There were to be generations and generations . . . who were to choose for themselves whether or not they were to be included in the sacrifice of Christ, and become acceptable to God by offering themselves with Christ to the heavenly Father.

41

Excerpt from a Homily (June 6, 2021) by Pope Francis

God makes himself tiny, like a morsel of bread. That is precisely why we need a great heart to be able to recognize, adore, and receive him. God's presence is so humble, hidden, and often unseen that, in order to recognize his presence, we need a heart that is ready, alert and welcoming. But if our heart, rather than a large room, is more a like a closet where we wistfully keep things from the past, or an attic where we long ago stored our dreams and enthusiasm, or a dreary chamber filled only with us, then it will be impossible to recognize God's silent and unassuming presence.

✠

VII. Order of Service

42

Sample Order of Service for a Lay-Led Holy Hour

Praying with and before Christ in the Eucharist is a gift for both individuals and communities, and lay-led Holy Hours continue to grow in popularity and practice. While there is no blessing without an ordained minister, lay ministers can expose and repose the Blessed Sacrament.

Opening Prayer

Can be chosen from numbers 1–22 or freely composed. The lay minister might also use this time to welcome all gathered.

Exposition of the Blessed Sacrament

The lay minister should remove the blessed sacrament from the tabernacle, place the blessed sacrament in the monstrance, and reverence the blessed sacrament with genuflection.

Allow time for silent reflection.

Reading I

Can be chosen from numbers 23–38, or any passage from Scripture.

Allow time for silent reflection.

Reading II

Can be chosen from numbers 23–28, or any passage from Scripture.

Allow time for silent reflection.

Litany

Can be prayed from number 22.

The Lord's Prayer

Reposition of the Blessed Sacrament

The lay minister should reverence the blessed sacrament with genuflection, remove the blessed sacrament from the monstrance, and place the blessed sacrament in the tabernacle.

Closing Prayer

Can be chosen from numbers 1–22 or freely composed.

Note: You may also wish to begin and end the Holy Hour with a hymn or song.

Acknowledgments

Scripture texts in this work are taken from the *New American Bible, revised edition* © 2010, 1991, 1986, 1970 Confraternity of Christian Doctrine, Washington, DC and are used by permission of the copyright owner. All rights reserved. No part of the New American Bible may be reproduced in any form without permission in writing from the copyright owner.

"Canticle of Zechariah," "Canticle of Mary," "Canticle of Simeon," "Psalm 23: The Lord Is My Shepherd," "Psalm 27: The Lord Is My Light and My Salvation," "Psalm 34: Taste and See the Goodness of the Lord," "Psalm 51: Have Mercy on Me, O God," and "Psalm 139: I Praise You, for I Am Wonderfully Made" from *The Abbey Psalms and Canticles* by the Monks of Conception Abbey © 2018, 2010 United States Conference of Catholic Bishops, Washington, DC. All rights reserved.

“Prayers before the Eucharist” and “Litany of the Holy Eucharist” taken from *Order for the Solemn Exposition of the Holy Eucharist* © 1992 United States Conference of Catholic Bishops, Washington, DC. All rights reserved.

“Penitential Prayer” from the English translation of *The Order of Penance* © 2019 International Commission on English in the Liturgy Corporation (ICEL). All rights reserved.

Excerpt from a homily (June 6, 2021) by Pope Francis © Dicastero per la Comunicazione-Libreria Editrice Vaticana. Used with permission.

“God Has Called Us” by Sister Thea Bowman, FSPA, from *Sister Thea Bowman, Shooting Star*, reprinted with permission from the Franciscan Sisters of Perpetual Adoration, fspa.org.

“Prophets of a Future Not Our Own” by Bishop Kenneth Untener © Little Books of the Diocese of Saginaw. Used with permission.

Excerpt from “You Are Yourselves What You Receive” from *The Works of Saint Augustine: A Translation for the*

21st Century, translated by Edmund Hill, OP, and edited by John E. Rotelle, OSA, published by New City Press, Hyde Park, NY, 1993. Used with permission.

Every effort was made to seek out the proper attributions and permissions for the texts contained in this edition. We apologize for any inadvertent omissions and, if informed in writing, will make corrections for future editions.